MEDIEVAL LIFE ILLUSTRATIONS

SELECTED AND ARRANGED BY

Carol Belanger Grafton

DOVER PUBLICATIONS, INC.
New York

Bibliographical Note

Medieval Life Illustrations is a new work, first published by Dover Publications, Inc., in 1996.

DOVER *Pictorial Archive* SERIES

Library of Congress Cataloging-in-Publication Data

Medieval life illustrations : selected and arranged / by Carol Belanger Grafton.
     p.   cm. — (Dover pictorial archive series)
  Includes bibliographical references.
  ISBN 0-486-28862-5 (pbk.)
  1. Civilization. Medieval—Pictorial works. 2. Middle Ages—Pictorial works.
I. Grafton, Carol Belanger. II. Series.
CB351.M3925 1996
909.07′022′2—dc20   95-40673
                                   CIP

Manufactured in the United States of America
Dover Publications, Inc., 31 East 2nd Street, Mineola, N.Y. 11501

PUBLISHER'S NOTE

THE ILLUSTRATIONS IN incunabula (books printed before 1501) provide an invaluable record of life in the latter part of the Middle Ages. Although many of the pictures are of a fabulous, historic or religious nature, the artists have incorporated details that reveal much about life during the period.

Most of the illustrations on these pages have been reproduced from *Der Bilderschmuck der Frühdrucke* (20 vols.), edited by Albert Schramm and published in Leipzig during the 1920s and 30s. Other illustrations were taken from reproductions in various nineteenth-century publications.

CONTENTS

Men and Women 1

Wealth and Royalty 10

Knights and Military Scenes 16

Eating, Drinking and Viticulture 24

Farming and Gardening 32

Laborers and Workers 40

Architecture and Landscapes 48

Merchants and Tradesmen 58

Games, Amusements and Tournaments 66

Music 70

Books and Scholars 74

Religion and Astrology 78

Medicine 82

Maritime Themes 84

Fish and Fishing 88

Hunting 92

Birds and Bees 96

Animals 105

Snakes, Serpents and Dragons 114

Fire 116

Violence and Death 118

Miscellaneous 120

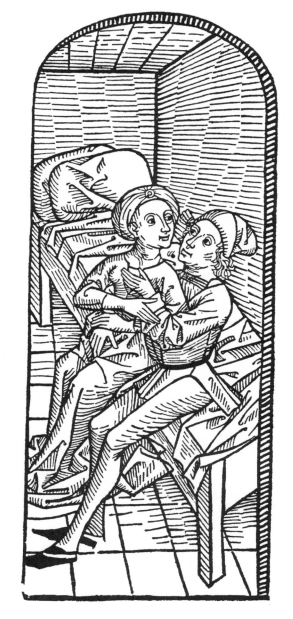

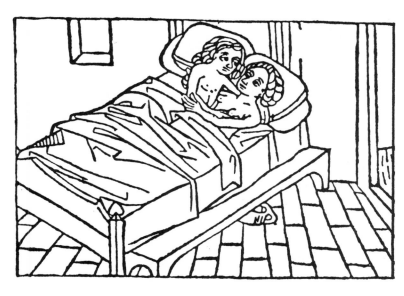

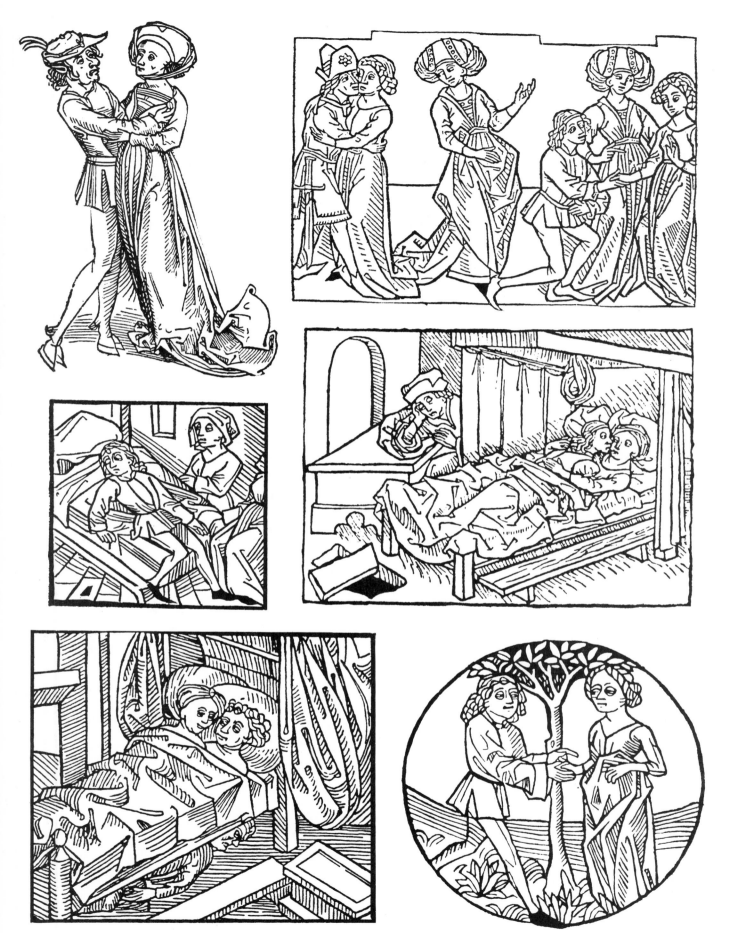

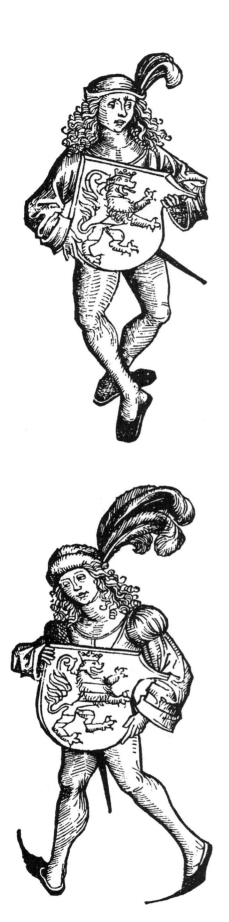

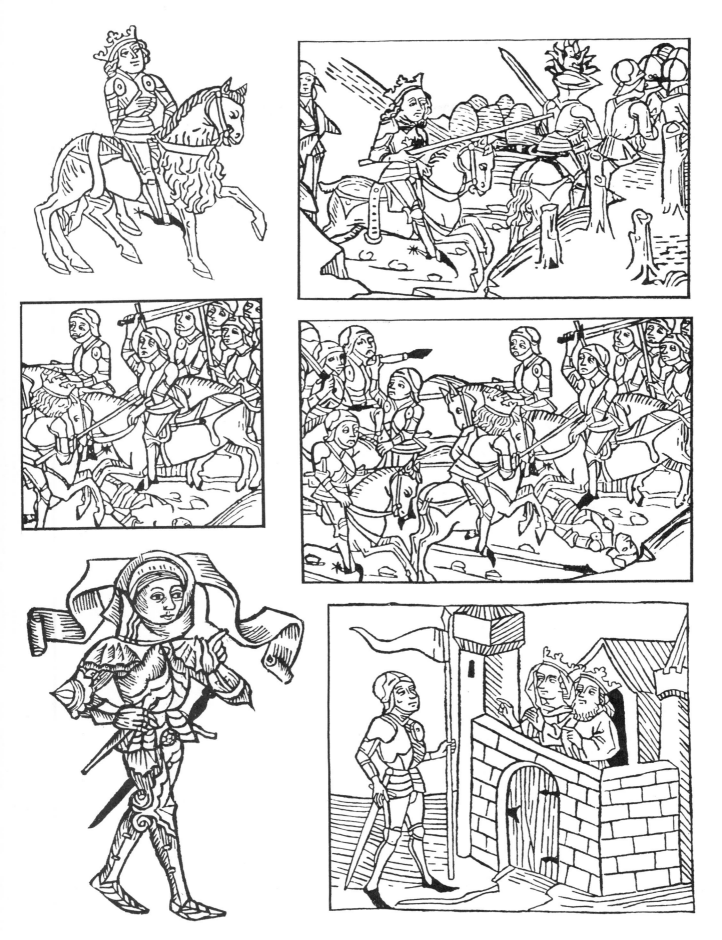

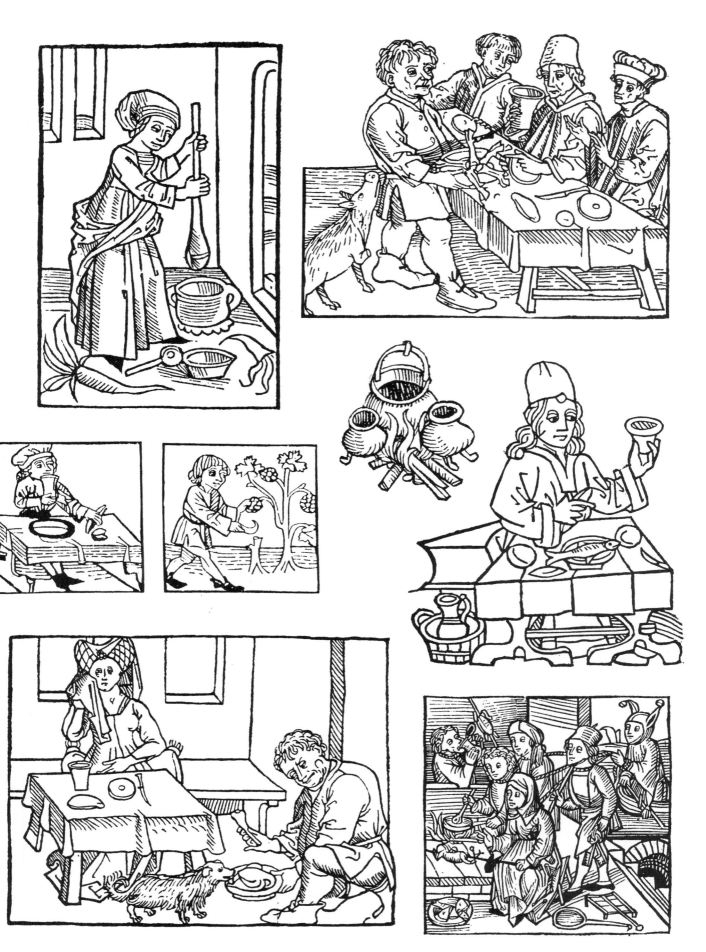

Plate 1

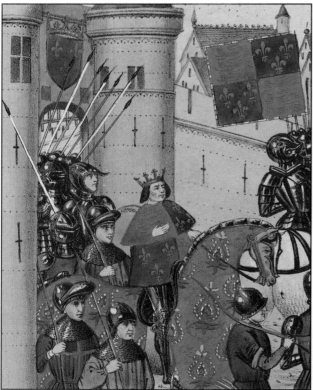 

Plate 2

Plate 3

Plate 4

Plate 5

Plate 6

Plate 7

Plate 8

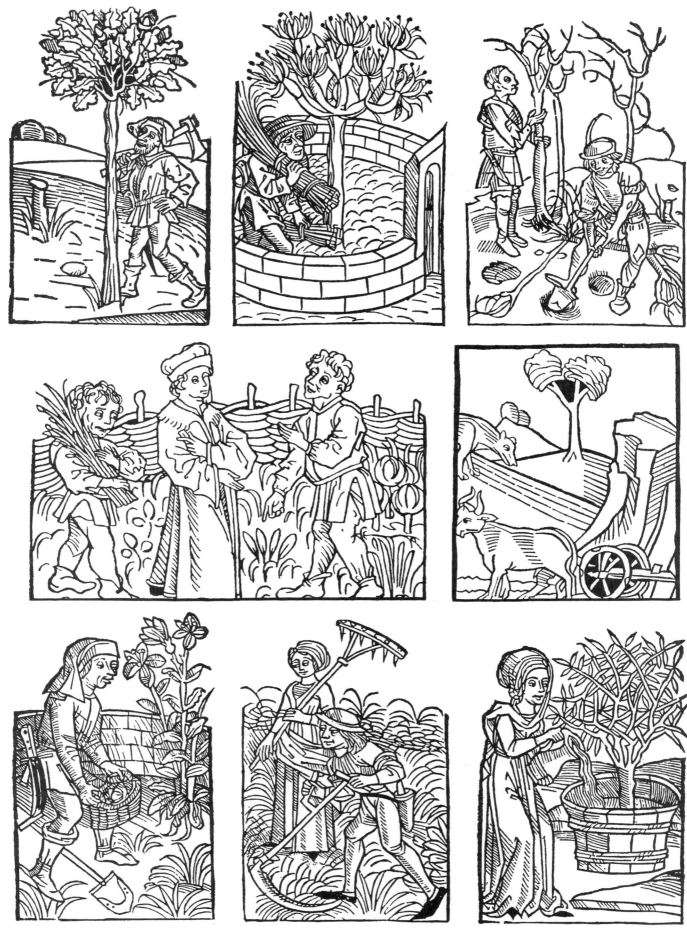

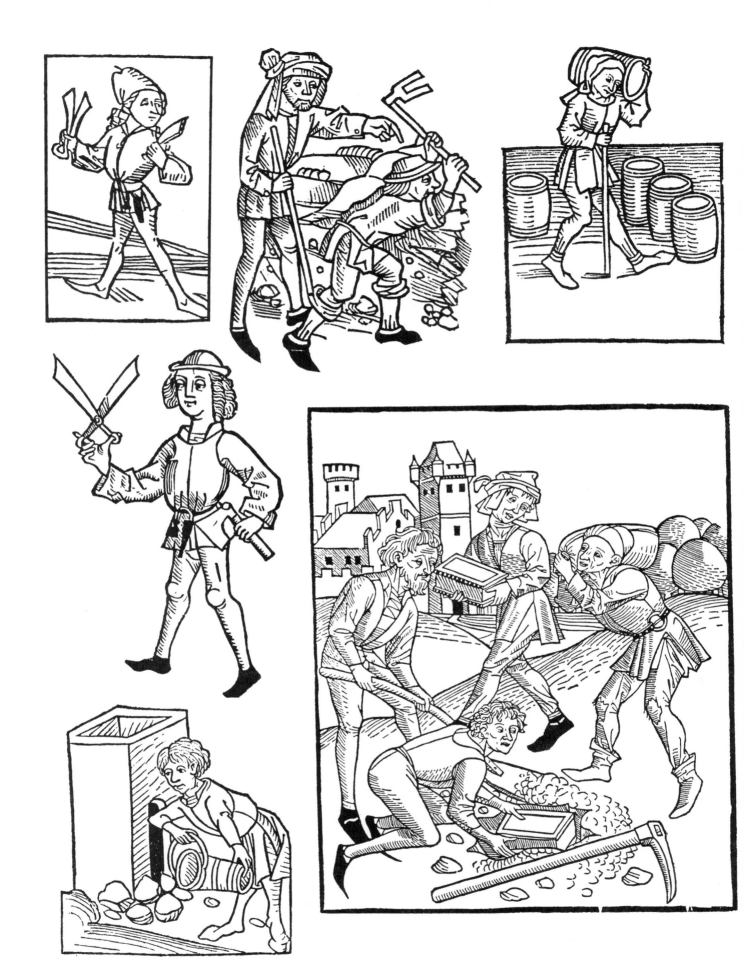

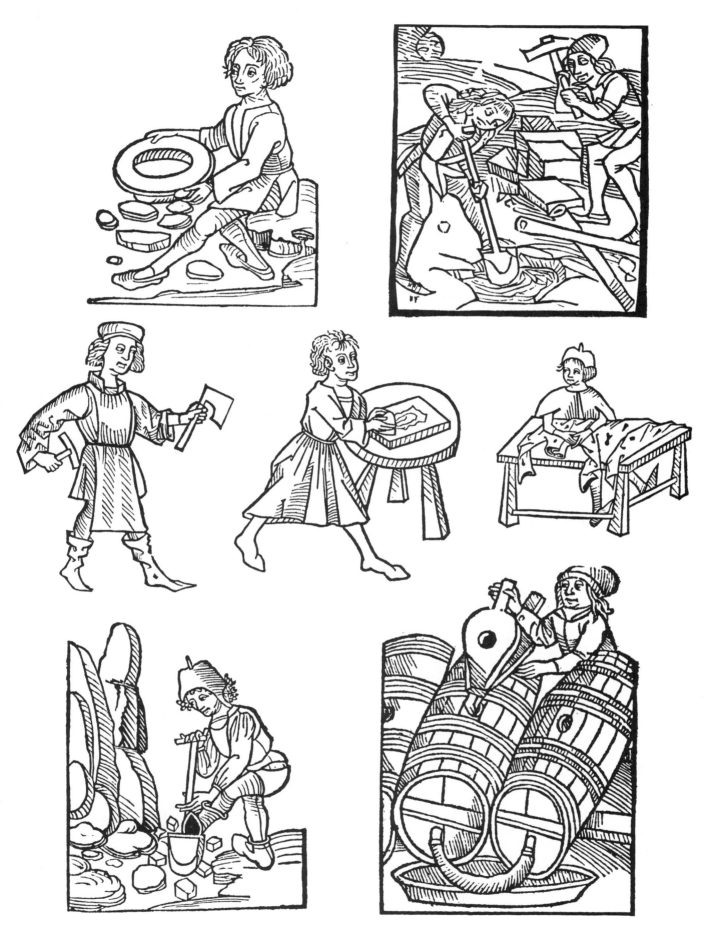

MERCHANTS AND TRADESMEN

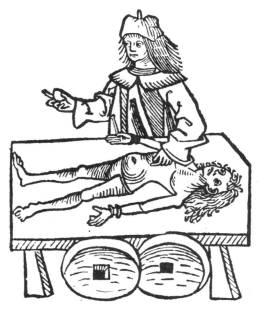

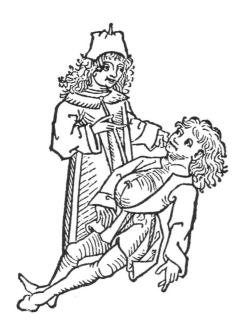

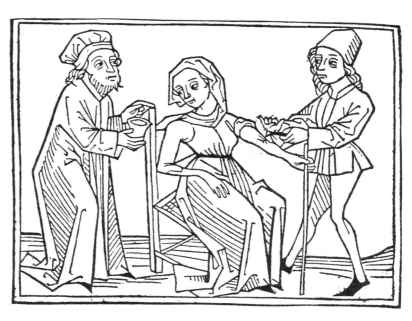

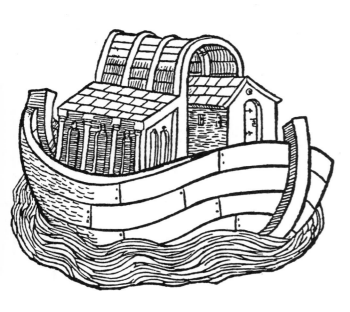

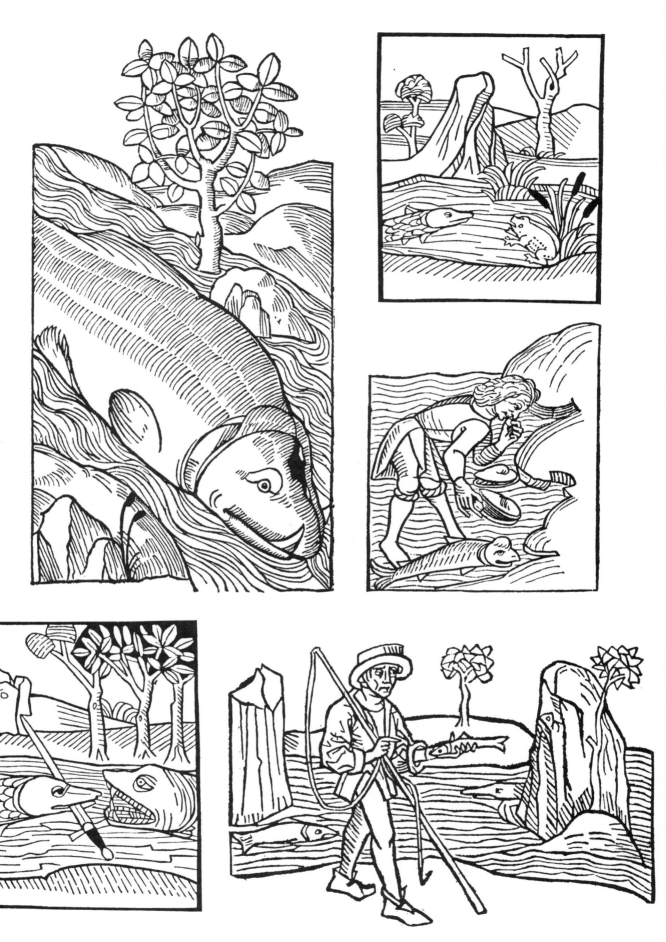

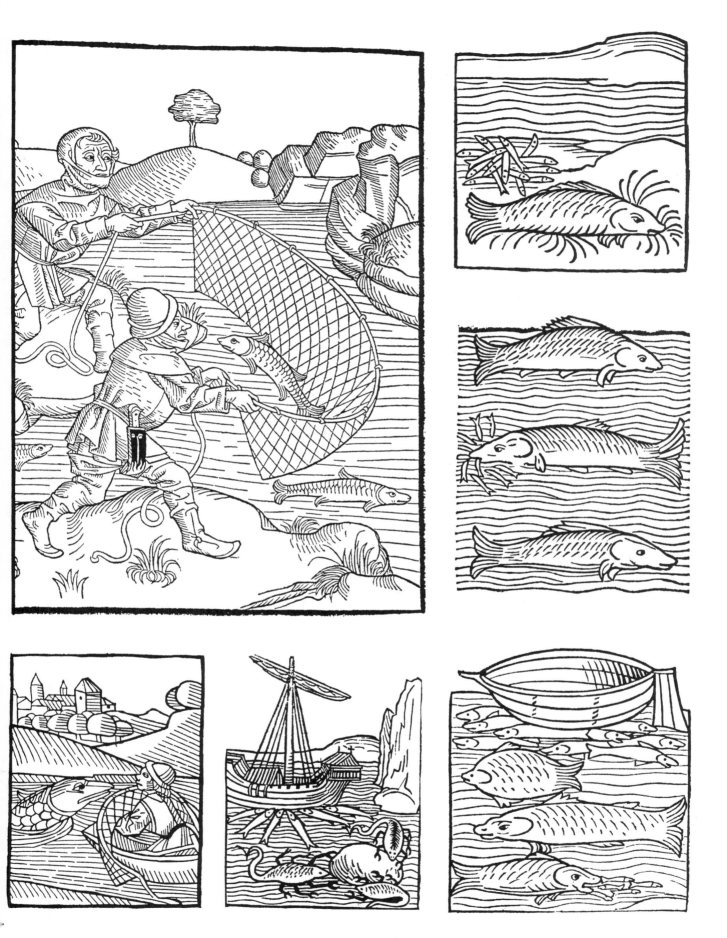

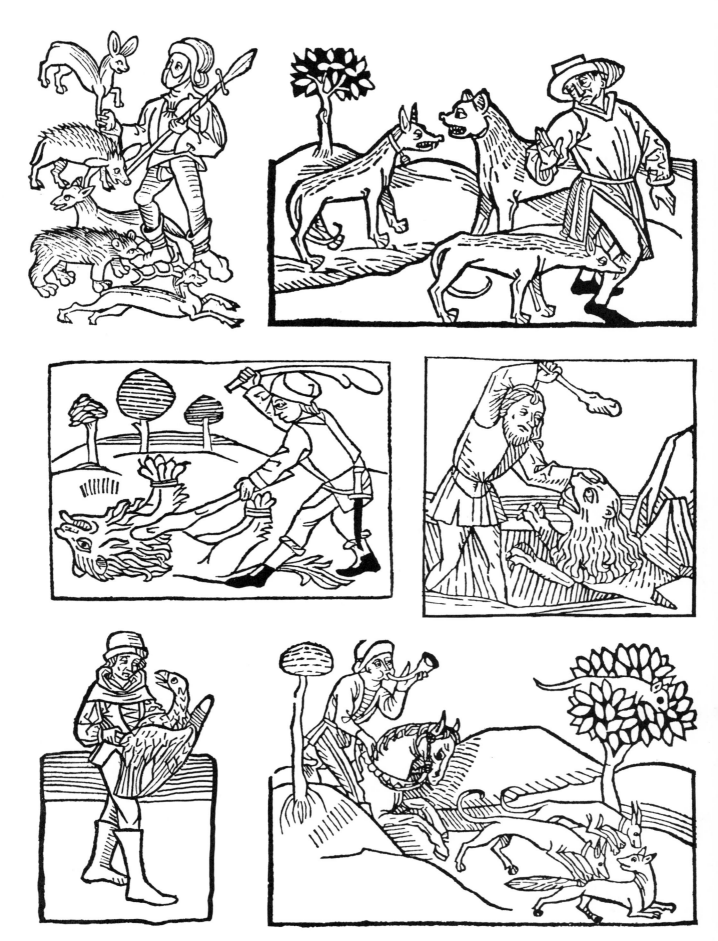

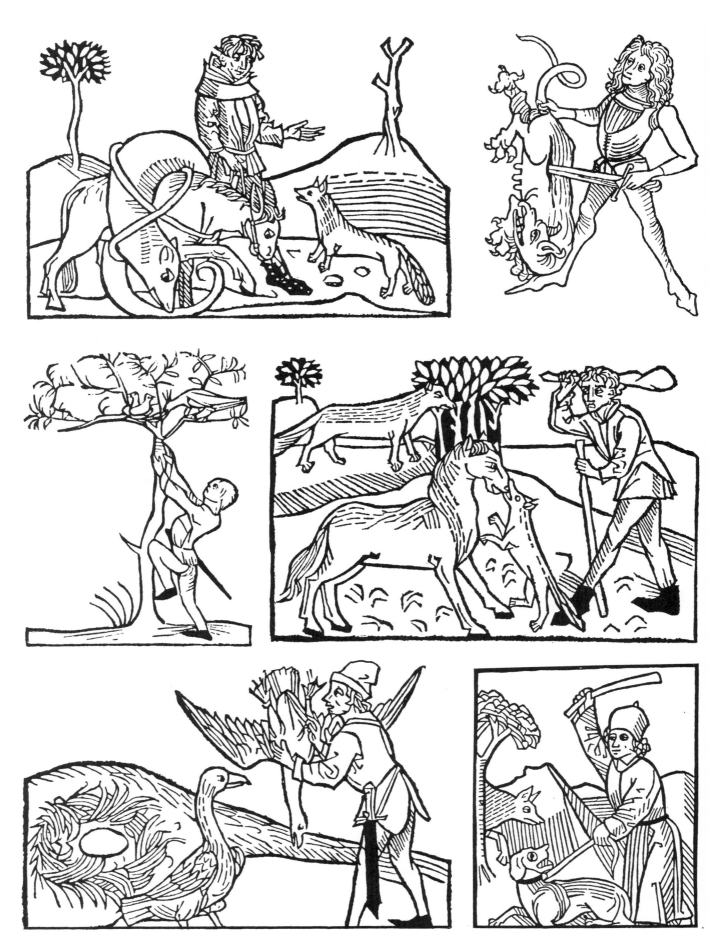

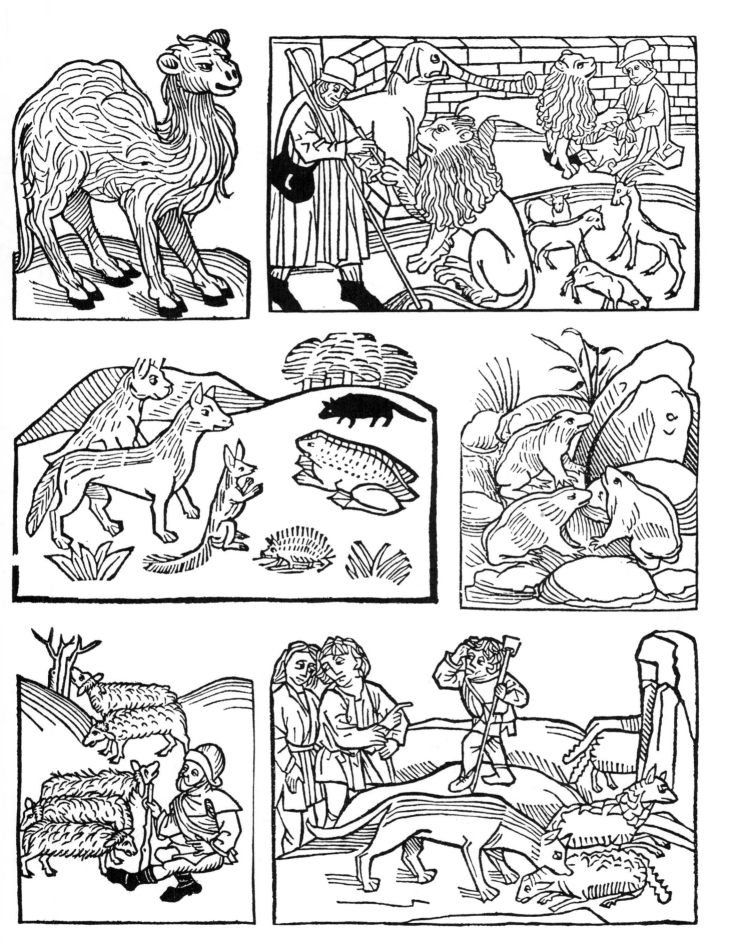

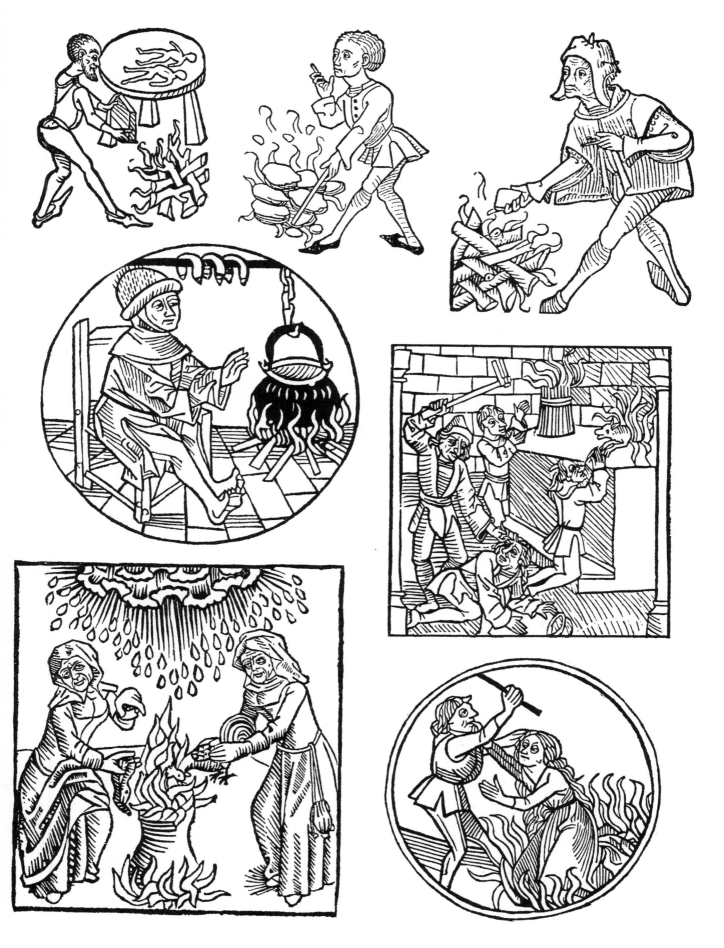

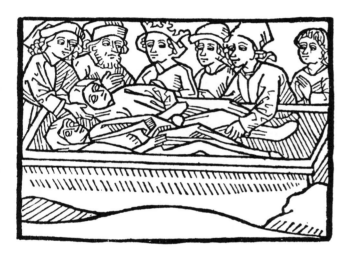

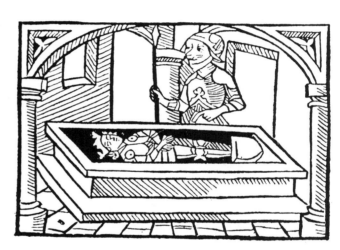